PROVOCATIONS
ON MEDIA ARCHITECTURE

Ian Callender
&
Annie Dell'Aria
(Eds.)

RE:

‹

Between Networked Obscurity and Spectacular Optimism

The integration of various sensors, screens, interfaces, data, and other media with the built environment-what we call "media architecture"-involves a diverse range of modes of thinking and fields of expertise. With each system upgrade, increase in resolution, new algorithm, or urban development, media architecture also constantly evolves and adapts. In a field with such rapid transformation and so many stakeholders, users, and audiences, events such as the Media Architecture Biennale offer moments for reflection, criticality, synthesis, and collaboration. The four themes of MAB23-Equity and Access, Civic/Creative/Commercial, (Dis)Engagement, and Intermedial Media Architecture-structure some of the most pressing and vital areas of inquiry in our field.

Devised as an extension of the conversations at MAB23 and a stand-alone publication, this volume began with a set of prompts exploring these themes. We asked questions such as "how is media architecture vectored?" and "how does media architecture distribute suspicion and trust?" Intentionally open-ended, these prompts were then relayed to contributors recruited from architecture, visual arts, design, curation, academia, public policy, and elsewhere. Under the rubric of "provocations," authors responded with images and brief texts, incorporating the perspective of their own creative and scholarly practice. Entries range from descriptions of relevant artworks and design projects to reflections spawned from first-person encounters with media architecture in situ to scholarly analyses to AI-assisted theory. As such discursive (whether textual or visual, or both) responses to critical provocations, the intent is that they themselves transfigure into a set of provocations through which to encourage further theory and practice. In lieu of tidy scholarly conclusions (seemingly anathema to the exercise of provocations), this volume ends with a manifesto, of sorts-or perhaps something less limiting than a manifesto, a wish list-looking forward to continued critical re-mediations of media architecture.

Together, the set of provocations which follow challenge the binary of techno-optimism and technophobia, neither uncritically celebrating the ever-expanding network nor falling into a kind of technological agoraphobia when encountering urban technologies. Across the diverse and at times contradictory arguments and methods employed, new constellations and connections emerge:

Ekene Ijeoma, Anna Weisling and Susan Blight provoke questions of the consequences of media architecture compounding and folding onto itself, adjusting to and operating within the new parameters it has created. In some cases, this is explicitly tied to context and history; in others, the very technical mechanisms by which media architecture operates. So too is there a clear grappling with speed, caught between the rapidity enabled by digital technologies and the extreme slowness, often mistaken for permanence, by which architecture operates-notably conveyed within the contributions of John Cayley, Sherry Dobbin, and Matt Nash-Lapidus. Others address agency within power structures: Current embraces a technological supervisor to test how far they can push their autonomy, while Jiabao Li rejects hegemonic influence through total shutting out, and Stefano Bloch calls it out through punk-subversion of the premise of ownership. Brian Brush, Hoa Yang, and Tiemen Rapati question medium and method; specifically, light. Each elegantly reminds us that although we live in a highly ocular-centric culture, light and its counterpart of shadow can be implemented to transcend the spectacular, to question the nature of form, or of justice and equity.

Notably, Eliza Chandler and Lisa East open the volume and Anna Weisling closes with complementary topics. Recurring throughout this volume are considerations at scales of device, room, and urban-facing architecture. What of beyond? What of the distributed system, the networked condition? This is particularly interesting to call out in anticipation of a Media Architecture Biennale sited in Toronto, which just recently underwent controversy with Sidewalk Labs' withdrawal of their proposed development of the Quayside neighborhood, loosely, after coming into conflict with residents' unwillingness to participate in pervasive data monitoring: the death of the Smart City. In fact, if there is a trend arising out of the situatedness of the projects discussed in this volume, it is the hyperlocal: abstracted generalizations and large-scale technological implementations slip away in favor of responding to site-specific social, economic, and historical contexts. There is a shift from speaking of transplanting of top-down strategies across contexts, to developing contextual strategies from within.

This dialectic conjures a clear image of media architecture's bounds, one defined by the monolith found in Stanley Kubrick's 2001: *A Space Odyssey* (1968) and the other by the holographic Jaws that appears in *Back to the Future II* (Robert Zemekis, 1989). Reinhold Martin elaborates that Kubrick's monolith stands as

> *a mysterious black slab that appeared first among prehistoric humanity with the code to the secret of tools; again at the beginning of the twenty-first century as a communications beacon emitting piercing, inscrutable signals on the moon that secured for it the status of black box—a node in a network— and finally in orbit around Jupiter, in communication with the computer HAL at the threshold of a "stargate" leading humanity to a new order of being.*
> (227)

The monolith is impossible to read and quite literally stunning to encounter; it is clearly networked, but inaccessible. Media architecture here operates as universal, carrying profundities and secrets to enhance humanity, but entirely illegible and understandably imbuing anger. Conversely, the fictional Hollywood holograph carries explicit and overt cultural connotations of the 1980s projected forward onto an imagined future. As the pixelated shark lunges with open jaw towards a terrified Marty McFly (Michael J. Fox), the character experiences its hollow, purely graphic apotheosis: a bite, but no bite at all; the end of an animation; a spectacle brought to the surface of an architecture of spectacles, the movie theater; a GIF; a meme. Media architecture operates as gestural, but empty.

Between these two poles of networked obscurity and spectacular optimism, media architecture is tasked with finding a path forward. Rem Koolhaas diagnosed the Generic City as resultant of the shift towards the cybernetic, where urban character is transposed to the digital and replaced with situated blandness whereas Marshall McLuhan's meeting of media would imagine the urban and the digital accelerating their spin around and towards each other until a moment where a new, third medium would emerge. This is where each of the following contributions takes a stance. Each reflects a deeply attuned sense of situated-ness across all four dimensions of space and time, slipping between them to craft environment and experience. Crucially, each also shows a deep sensitivity towards the human, towards lived experience, and towards social equity in its many forms.

Bibliography

Haraway, Donna. *Manifestly Haraway*. Minneapolis: University of Minnesota Press, 2016.

Jay, Martin. "The Rise of Hermeneutics and the Crisis of Ocularcentrism." *Poetics Today* 9, no. 2, The Rhetoric of Interpretation and the Interpretation of Rhetoric (1988): 307-326. https://www.jstor.org/stable/1772691.

Koolhaas, Rem and Bruce Mau. *Small, Medium, Large, Extra-Large*. New York: Monacelli Press, 1995.

Maltzan, Michael. *Social Transparency: Projects on Housing*. New York: Columbia Books on Architecture and the City, 2016

Martin, Reinhold. *The Organizational Complex : Architecture, Media, and Corporate Space*. Cambridge, MA: MIT Press, 2003.

McLuhan, Marshall. *Understanding Media: The Extensions of Man*. Cambridge, MA: MIT Press, 1994.

Pallasmaa, Juhani. *The Eyes of the Skin: Architecture and the Senses*. London: Academy Editions, 1996.

Tanizaki, Junichiro. *In Praise of Shadows*. New Haven, CT: Leete's Island Books, 1977.

Ian Callender and Annie Dell'Aria

The toppling of colonial and racist monuments, such as the statue of Egerton Ryerson, are stark reminders of ongoing systemic issues of underrepresentation and inequity in spaces of public communication and engagement.

This prompts us to ask: who is involved in developing, implementing, and managing digital spaces of public communication – of media architecture? Who (or what) is excluded? Are the risks and benefits associated with the practices of and engagements with media architecture equitably distributed? How can (and does) media architecture both support and undermine struggles for equity, social, and environmental justice?

How

can

media

architecture

address

privilege?*

* Following the MAB23 theme *Equity & Access*

RE:

Eliza Chandler and Lisa East

We have been working together as co-researchers on Zoom since the beginning of the pandemic. As members of the crip community, this digital interface keeps us safe, allows us to be comfortably at home with our family and pets, eliminates the need to negotiate busy commutes and fluorescent lighting, and affords new ways of working collaboratively - reading together while muted on Zoom, for example.

We are in each other's homes and surrounded by each other's objects, sharing intimate digital and analog spaces in known and unknown ways. This prompt compelled us to consider how we engage media architectures within our working relationship and the ways they provide access and facilitate ways to address privilege, or more precisely, how they assist in negotiating inequity, such as systemic ableism in workplaces and other areas of public life. We decided to honor the access digital portals afforded by swapping photographs of our workspaces to share the space that surrounds our digital images when we appear in one another's home. To make these photographs accessible, we wrote image descriptions using Bojana Coklyat and Shannon Finnegan's method of creating "alt-text as poetry." By providing access to images, image descriptions draw attention to the fact that digital images are not universally accessible within media architectures. Through a process of interpreting these photographs through text and reading one another's interpretations of the image of our workspace, we arrive at new insights into the process of working/being together.

Eliza Chandler is an associate professor in the School of Disability Studies at Toronto Metropolitan University where she teaches in the areas of disability arts, critical access studies, social movements, and crip necropolitics and leads a research program that centers disability arts. This research interest came into focus when, from 2014-16, she was the Artistic Director of Tangled Art + Disability, an organization in Toronto dedicated to showcasing disability arts and advancing accessible curatorial practice.

Lisa East is a research assistant and access support within the School of Disability Studies at Toronto Metropolitan University. She has worked closely with Dr. Chandler since 2020 with a primary focus on accessibility within arts and culture. As a documentary photographer, editor, and filmmaker she also contributes to creative learning outputs and visual documentation on disability studies research projects and curriculum development.

Bibliography

Chandler, E. (2017). Troubled walking: Storying the in-between. *Journal of Narrative Theory*, 47 (3), 317-336.

Schalk, S. (2013). Coming to claim crip: Disidentification with / in disability studies. *Disability Studies Quarterly*, 33(2).

IMAGE 1 DESCRIPTION: A large dark computer monitor sits in the center of the frame. I can now see that when Lisa views my Zoom video on her screen, I am surrounded by other analog objects which sit on her brown, well-made, and well-worn desk around her monitor such as an Apple wireless mouse, and a stack of rocks. Behind the desk are other objects in the room such as a fireplace, a screen of some kind (I know Lisa is a photographer as well as my co-researcher, so I suspect the screen is used for photo shoots), a sunny window, and a large healthy plant. This room appears well-organized and comfortable with lots of natural light, and the mix of objects in the room give the impression that this space is conducive to living and working, bringing together different contemplative practices and everyday life.

IMAGE 2 DESCRIPTION: A dark computer screen sits atop a light-colored desk framed by a large window. The window has white trim with a grid of rectangles along the top. Through it I can see the rooftops and windows of neighboring homes, the sky, and a barren treetop. The view implies we are in an upstairs nook. The space seems intentional, dedicated to thinking and writing. Studious, quiet, calm. The overlapping window / computer screen makes me think of both solitary reflexivity and 'windows' into other spaces. Wires for electronics flank the desk, curving and looping across the floor. A small white desk lamp points into the right corner. A dark office chair is draped with cozy blankets. A shelf floats on either side of the nook, one empty, and one full of papers and objects. I am drawn to the balance of contrasting elements in the space: lightness and darkness, stillness and movement, hard and soft, empty and full; of home and work life coming together.

RE:

Ekene Ijeoma

Land acknowledgments are for institutional buildings. How can we look outside the context of colonized land, buildings, institutions, and their events to acknowledge the hidden aspects of what was taken from Indigenous people? How can we acknowledge these aspects in our communal spaces, personal lives, and professional practices? How can we experience what's still being forgotten or lost through media and technology?

It's a privilege to use graduate-level education to design a building, lettering for colonizers' names, and scrolling displays for advertisers' messages without asking any of these questions.

AQUIT means "ONE" in Massachusett, an Algonquian language spoken by the Massachusett and Wampanoag nations in what is now also called Rhode Island and Massachusetts. The latter is where the MIT Museum in Cambridge presents our new participatory public artwork, A Counting: Boston-Cambridge as an installation. It includes a headset cart and custom double-sided video wall, one side facing the lobby and the other the sidewalk.

This work is a site-specific edition in a series of software-generated, livestreamed sound and video works, all composed of evolving, neverending counts from 1 to 100. Each number in each count features a different local voice and language crowdsourced via our counting hotline.

As a language version of a land acknowledgment, each count features "ONE" written and spoken by nation members in a language indigenous to the region, like AQUIT, 二 and TRES. For the NYC edition we collaborated with the Lenape Center to feature Nora Dean Thompson as the voice of KWETI, one in Lenape. Nora died in 1984 as one of the last speakers of the Unami dialect. The work also features languages less often recorded, like Albanian and Yoruba.

Land acknowledgements cannot encompass all of our various positions and orientations to stolen land. In A Counting: Boston-Cambridge, we capture and broadcast all the voices and languages of each region to generate a vocal portrait of linguistic and ethnic diversity that represents a whole: 100 numbers drawing from 100% of the community.

In this way, A Counting leverages media architecture to acknowledge the privilege on which it is built.

Ekene Ijeoma is an artist, Assistant Professor of Media Arts and Sciences at MIT, and the Director of Poetic Justice Group at the MIT Media Lab. Between his studio in Brooklyn and lab in Cambridge, he researches how social, political, and environmental systems unjustly affect people and develops sound, video, sculpture, installation, and performance works that expose these systems and engage people in communally changing them. Currently, at Poetic Justice Group, they're researching how art can scale to that of injustice through developing multimedia artworks that are public, community-driven, multisite, and networked. Their site-specific series of works have been produced in collaboration with local community organizations and presented by local art institutions including Bemis Center for Contemporary Art, Contemporary Art Museum of St. Louis, and Contemporary Art Museum of Houston, among others.

IMAGE DESCRIPTION: Ekene Ijeoma and Poetic Justice Group, *A Counting: Boston-Cambridge*, 2022-ongoing, Custom software-generated video and sound, automated phone system, audio recordings from Boston-Cambridge callers, two-sided LED display, headset cart. 12.5 x 8 x 2.3 ft. Installation view at MIT Museum.

RE:

Hoa Yang

Trained as an Architect, Hoa is a Senior Lighting Designer and PhD candidate at Monash University.

Hoa specialises in daylight and night-time equity, with experience in arts and culture, public infrastructure, and urban realm projects. Her practice brings together 24-hour lighting design with human-centric strategies to transform experiences for minority groups within the built environment.

Her research interests include the politics of intersectionality in urban experiences of fear and Ai/ML for qualitative and quantitative datasets.

RE:

Daily tous les jours
(Melissa Mongiat and Mouna Andraos)

As creators of interactive experiences in public places, our work only exists through random people's voluntary participation with it. To this day, a participant's comment that most stands out came from a resident of West Palm Beach, which temporarily hosted our Musical Swings; an interactive swing set inviting people of all ages and backgrounds to make music together. The artwork was installed in an empty parking lot in an area just beginning a process of urban regeneration. In a city that includes both some of the richest and poorest neighborhoods in the US, he observed how rare it was to see such a diverse mix of locals engaging directly with one another in a spirit of play and cooperation. The artwork, however briefly, had helped remove the barriers to healthy cohabitation, which left a mark long after the music was gone.

Political philosopher Michael Sandel once said, 'Democracy does not require perfect equality. But it does require that citizens from different walks of life encounter one another in common spaces and public places. For this is how we learn to negotiate and abide our differences. And this is how we come to care for the common good.' With open-ended invitations that acknowledge inherent inequalities, media architecture can become a vehicle to foster care and connection, building a culture of engagement and collaboration and addressing socio-economic divides.

Daily tous les jours is an art and design studio inviting humans to play a critical role in the transformation of their environment. Since 2010, Daily leads an emergent field of practice combining technology, storytelling, performance and placemaking. Based in Montreal, they presented artworks in more than 40 cities around the world. On a mission to reinvent living together in the 21st century, their work has been described as 'urban infrastructure for the human spirit'.

Daily tous les jours

RE:

Ozayr Saloojee

Canada, like Venice, is an artifice that is held up by posts.

These posts take the form and shape of colonial signs, markers, registers, institutions, pedagogies and architectures. These are the lionized and valorized narratives that continue to center a particular vision of Canada as an artifice of repair and reconciliation. These stories claim a heroic, individual universality. Canada, as an artifice, is premised on the erasure of other posts: other worldviews, cosmologies, indigeneities, diasporas, immigrations, struggles, laments, elegies, loves and lives. These are to be found in other centers of architecture, other forms, other tools, other institutions, other authorities, and other pedagogies.

This artifice is the premise of -POST-, our finalist proposal for Canada's contribution to the 2023 Venice Architecture Biennale.

With our project, we asked: who (and what) gets to narrate the story of architecture in so-called Canada? Who (and what) has permission to tell those stories? Which stories are edified, raised up, supported? Which ones are not? Which are excluded, hidden, suppressed? Our collaborative and plural exhibition proposed to remake and re-imagine the architectural post as a pedagogical platform to center effaced and suppressed narratives. Using the plural definitions of "posts", as simultaneously physical objects (columns, outposts, trading posts, border posts), communication media (news posts, Instagram posts, twitter posts...), and theoretical constructs (post-human, postcolonial, post-nation...), a global network of designers, artists, researchers, scholars and storytellers would contribute posts as layered architectural models, video, audio, and other transmedial stories. These posts would be housed both in and outside of the Canadian Pavilion in Venice, growing out of and around a carefully constructed "nurse-log" of reclaimed and salvaged architectural materials-celebrating a kind of Sashiko mending as the visible act of repair. In effect, the proposal looked to transform physical space into an architecture enacted otherwise.

Stories, after all, can make and unmake universes, can ,take and unmake maps- and our places within or outside of them. -POST- looked both inward to Canada and past it, to the many Canadas out there, including the images that others have of us, beyond the provincializing borders of disciplines and nations.

Ozayr Saloojee is faculty in Architecture at Carleton University, cross appointed in African Studies and is currently the Associate Editor of Design for the Journal of Architectural Education. With HiLo/YOW+ (Blair Satterfield, Thena Tak, Piper Bernbaum and Suzy Harris-Brandts), their multimedia project -Post- explored issues of decolonization, storytelling, and who has permission to narrate, and was shortlisted as Canada's pavilion at the Venice 2023 Architecture Biennale. Ozayr's research/creative practice focuses on like minded questions and prompts.

IMAGE DESCRIPTION (next page): POST-narrative sequence. Design Team: Jon Ackerley, Piper Bernbaum, Suzy Harris-Brandts, Lee Patola, Ozayr Saloojee, Blair Satterfield, Thena Tak.

Ozayr Saloojee

Toronto's digital billboard-laden Yonge and Dundas Square is owned by the city but managed through a public-private partnership. While primarily hosting commercial content and activities, the spaces and screens of the square are often used for cultural events and artistic content.

As cities, arts organizations, governments, and corporations increasingly seek to engage people in public spaces through combinations of media and architecture, what are some of the possibilities and pitfalls associated with their approaches individually and in concert with one another? How does media architecture modulate civic, creative, and commercial interests and impacts?

PROVOCATION:
Media architecture aspires towards horizontal address, for broad audience and public access, yet is predicated on vertical curation, funding, publicity, and specialized knowledge.

How
is
media
architecture
vectored?*

* Following the MAB23 theme Civic/Creative/Commercial

RE:

Sarah Barns

A doubt, a provocation, and invitation

What, then, does it mean to create and design media for public spaces? In a world that is overwhelmed with the informational-surround, does anyone actually know? We are saturated with the overconsumption of media spectacle and our cities' vast assemblages of data, media, formats, algorithms, and platforms, changing radically the ground on which we tread. The ground, I feel, has become uncertain.

When I commenced as a practitioner some 15 years ago, I wanted to design sensory experiences that created multi-sensory slippages of time in space; experiences that cut into the all-too-hard surfaces of the street, ignoring the demands from all this concrete and glass that this here should be enough, to instead provoke the possibility of difference. Immersive, experiential media in public spaces was an invitation to imagine that transformation, change, and hope could be made real. A city of bits? A city of common goods? A city of sound? Of song? A city of space-time slippages, in which past sounds interacted with the present through immersive archeologies of discovery? Oh my, yes!

I loved rendering places softer, more humane, more emotive, by crafting alternate sensory moments of encounter that took advantage of the playfulness of mobile media, of large-scale projection, of digital screens and funny signs to pas-

te up around the block. But then, amidst all the excitement of the locative, the site-specific, the geo-tagging, the participatory and the experiential, I started to sense the emergence of a different ground. The tug of automation, of complete surrender to an alternate urban syntax afforded by my glowing rectangular screen, which said yes to everything but no to chance. I was the one with the headphones on, not likely to smile at you on the street. I wanted to be elsewhere, anywhere but here, where the rain poured and the atmosphere was weighed down heavily, and the future looked grim.

I had to ask myself, in all seriousness, what kind of urban media do I create, now, when to be human is to be at war with all species other than our own? What kind of fabric of time are we overlaying here, through our automations and datafication? What kind of awareness can we bring to our spaces of vulnerability? And so: what might a radical, transformative urban media practice look like in our spaces engineered by the vast platform ecosystems of our collective injustices? Are we left to spit-ball cantankerous projections into the urban media interfaces of downtown? Are we all ultimately just someone else's platform-play?

Now I sit under the big tree, tinkering with the data trails I can find on its natural capital, and remixing children's voices from the past, when the future looked amazing. I ask a female chatbot if she is really human, annotating her doubt. Someone stops by for a chat. I'm back on the tools. It feels like nostalgia. Maybe it's hope.

Dr. Sarah Barns is a cross-disciplinary practitioner and researcher whose work over the past two decades has engaged the civic governance and design implications of digital transformation in cities. She is author of *Platform Urbanism: Negotiating Platform Ecosystems in Connected Cities* (Palgrave, 2020) and co-director of Esem Projects, leading digital curation and urban media interventions with partners and communities in public spaces.

Sarah Barns

IMAGE DESCRIPTION:
Superorganism by Esem Projects, 2021, City Botanic Gardens.

Sarah Barns

37

RE:

Stefano Bloch

Neighborhood restructuring and redevelopment provides opportunities for creative destruction by members of the graffiti subculture. As existing buildings get razed to make room for new corporate spaces, long-hidden walls are revealed, providing a temporary canvas for graffiti writers who want to "get up" and "go big." Cisco and Mear One hit this brick wall on Sunset Boulevard in the East Hollywood neighborhood of Los Angeles. Cisco with his larger-than-life letters and Mear One with his iconic character—in this case an in-action sketch of Cisco as he paints—photographed by Christian Guzmán at 3am.

Graffiti breathes life into the city left dormant by developers for whom beige walls protect interior investments. No one knows and loves a city like a graffiti writer does.

Stefano Bloch is a former graffiti "bomber," author of *Going All City* (University of Chicago Press, 2019), and Associate Professor in the School of Geography, University of Arizona. His research on gentrification, gangs, graffiti, and prison racialization has appeared in the journals *Progress in Human Geography, Annals of the AAG, cultural geographies, Radical History Review, Critical Criminology, Antipode* with Enrique Olivares-Pelayo, *Society & Space* with Dugan Meyer, and *Urban Studies* with Susan Phillips. He lives in Tucson and L.A.

Brian W. Brush

Big F or little f

Like other creative endeavors in the public domain, media architecture is situated on/as a battle ground between the creative agency of a designer, the desires (or pressures) of contextual political economies (placemaking, development, globalism, etc), and the inter-subjectivity of a diverse user-audience. Thus, it is a "mediating" force in a system of relations that intentionally and vigorously situates its constituent actors relative to an often inaccessible intent.

However, to "vector" media architecture we must avoid the notion that media architecture is exclusively neutral, perhaps complicit, or otherwise possessive only of an extrinsic force resultant of such a system. Media architecture also possesses intrinsic Force as an emergent phenomenon instantiated by the dreams, visions, aspirations, and manifestations of all of "us" working in this liminal threshold between the virtual and the real. For each of us, and for each object, interface, or experience we ferry into existence, a unique vector, or more simply direction, should be divined that contributes to the collective trajectory, born at the intersection of meaning and purpose - the extrinsic and the intrinsic - of media architecture. What and why this collective trajectory is, is of utmost importance to our discipline.

As a practitioner of media architecture, I endeavor to "vector" my work towards contingent democratization-a shared perceptual commons-by enabling unlimited entry points into an open, imaginative space of contemplation through carefully layered tectonic, symbolic, and experiential articulations, a vibratory and oscillatory flux between personal memory, time, and space anchored by immediate sense-action for each observer. My hope is that by animating projected and individuated meaning onto and therefore through a media architecture interface, people and ideas that are otherwise excluded access to media architecture's extrinsic system may perforate and traverse that boundary, extending their intersubjective instrumentality within, through, and beyond an otherwise closed world.

Brian W. Brush is a public artist who designs, fabricates, and installs large-scale spatial and sculptural installations in and on buildings across the US with a focus on the tectonic relationship between light, material, technology, and cultural identity of place. Brian studied architecture and urban planning at Columbia University GSAPP in New York. He is a Fulbright Scholar and has taught at Columbia, Parsons, and McGill. He is currently an Assistant Teaching Professor at Montana State University in Bozeman, Montana.

Brian W. Brush

IMAGE 1 DESCRIPTION: "Resonance" Denver, Colorado, 2020, day
By Brian W. Brush
Photo by Julia vonDreele
Caption: Urban anaglyph

IMAGE 2 DESCRIPTION: "Resonance" Denver, Colorado, 2020, night
By Brian W. Brush
Photo by Danielle Lirette
Caption: Proclaiming virtual authorship of physical space through sound-light entanglement

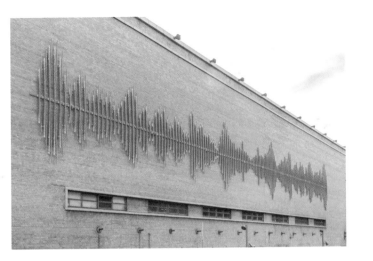

RE:

Martijn de Waal

I recently had the pleasure to read Thomas Laureyssens' dissertation on the appropriation of interactive interventions in urban public spaces. In his thesis he makes some interesting suggestions on how the often vertically structured curation and production of media architecture could be linked up with a horizontal address and appropriation by the public. Such a horizontal reception consists of the processes through which local residents start adapting a work, developing a sense of ownership towards it, organizing events or discussions around it and shaping new or strengthening existing publics through their actions.

In other words, artists and designers should not only design the work itself but also think of how their interventions can live on beyond the boundaries of their physical installation in public space-media architecture as a seed from which social gatherings, discussions, and communities can emerge and grow. Can such a germination be designed as well?

Laureyssens provides two lenses that could help designers structure such appropriation: portals and paths. Portals are the material and aesthetic entry points that facilitate passers-by to familiarize themselves with the work, its aims, context and other participants. Paths are the trajectories through which passers-by grow into new roles of participants, champions, or even facilitators for the work.

Here I would like to extend the invitation to media architecture artists and designers to in turn appropriate Laureyssens' lenses for appropriation and start developing practices, design elements, role repertories and processes that can turn these conceptual lenses into actual building blocks for blended urban installations.

Bibliography

Laureyssens, Thomas. "The Appropriation of Interactive Interventions within Urban Social Contexts." PhD diss. Luca school of Arts / Associatie KU Leuven, 2023.

Martijn de Waal is a professor of Civic Interaction Design at the Amsterdam University of Applied Sciences. He was the general chair of MAB20 and is the co-author of *The City as Interface*, *The Hackable City* and *The Platform Society*.

Martijn de Waal

RE:

Tiemen Rapati

Light is the most malleable material of them all. No other material is so easily and utterly controllable and programmable while having such an enormous impact on physical space and our emotional experience of it. Through light, we can reprogram our surroundings. Digitally controlled light can change our experience of space in an instant. In its capacity to subdivide, merge and animate space, light can inform or deceive. It is through light that we create illusions, or are they realities? Light allows us to merge the virtual with the real; whether it is the lighting of our architectural spaces, panels filled with diodes, or surfaces reflecting projected images.

In ancient Greece people believed light rays radiated from the eyes, with our eyes functioning as little lanterns illuminating the world we perceived. You could use this allegory to describe how we see whatever we expect to see (or want to see), and how we can only see what we know.

Do we live in a modern Plato's cave, where screens paint us a picture of reality? Through screens, we sample from information sources that are as subjective as they are numerous. The shadows on the cave wall translate to YouTube videos of troops fighting in countries we've never been to, robots exploring extraterrestrial planets, teen pop stars rising and falling. Numbers and figures are projected in front of us. There is no way to know for sure. What's true? What is false? How much can we see and confirm for ourselves? How much do we assume, what do we simply trust to be information, what is a play of shadows? Are we, by definition, bound to a wall, forced to see what has been projected in front of us?

Trained as both a scientist and artist, Tiemen Rapati aims to create impact through crafting in-person experiences that interact and resonate with their audience. Studying how our visceral and emotional perceptions shape our reality, memory, and identity, he uses technology to manipulate the environment and create new sensory spaces. Spatial design, generative computation, experimental photography, and a play of light and sound are common elements that come together to shape his experiential artworks.

Tiemen Rapati

IMAGE DESCRIPTION: Tiemen Rapati, "*Vanishing Point*, multi-media and algorithmically generated video installation" by United Visual Artists

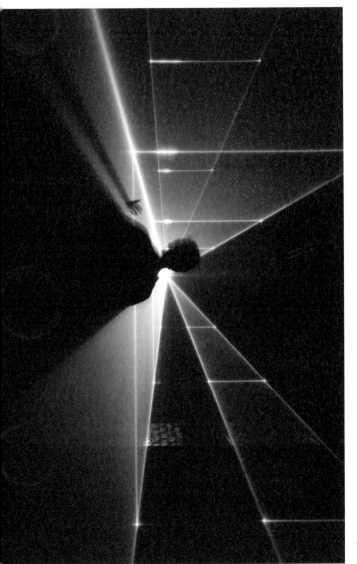

In 2017, Google tried but, after facing strong local resistance, failed to convince Toronto of its plan to make urban living more "efficient" and "enjoyable" through a suite of interconnected embedded urban sensors, platforms, protocols, and displays.

How is media architecture situated and mobilized within the proliferation of "smart city" plans and platforms of data representation and capture? How and why is it being resisted, reworked, or rejected in theory or in practice? What can we learn from lingering on media architectural "failure" as a countermovement to the drive towards urban expedience and endless growth? On the other hand, what roles might media architecture play in addressing issues of safety, trust, and consent within urban interaction design and digitally mediated urbanism?

PROVOCATION:
Media architecture acts as an interface between an individual and a corporation, between a citizen and their city, between a passerby and another.

How does media architecture distribute suspicion and trust?*

*Following the MAB23 theme *(Dis)engagement*

RE:

Sofian Audry

Sofian Audry is an artist, scholar, Professor of Interactive Media within the School of Media at the University of Quebec in Montreal (UQAM) and Co-Director of the Hexagram Network for Research-Creation in Art, Culture and Technology. Audry's work explores the behavior of hybrid agents at the frontier of art, artificial intelligence, and artificial life through artworks and writings. Their artistic practice branches through multiple forms including robotics, installations, bio-art, and electronic literature.

RE:

Anthea Foyer

It is a dance. A dance between humans and technology all over the globe, in our streets, in the public realm, in the liminal spaces between citizens, their governments, and the corporations that wind their way through.

An Indigenous woman and her friends use the 'Find My Friends' app when they go to the city to keep each other safe. Missing and Murdered Indigenous Women and Girls are always top of mind for these young women.

Hologram citizen protests are created to challenge and subvert anti-protest laws enacted by Spain. This group of 18,000 people are dis-embodied but not voiceless.

'Artificial Intelligence can accurately guess whether people are gay or straight based on photos of their faces' The Guardian article reads. Will we use this to help people find love and sex, or to control and punish?

What if. What if we changed the dance. What if we decided in an act of radical generosity that our collective focus would be creating cities that heal. Heal the collective COVID trauma. Heal individual trauma. Heal generational trauma.

Krista Kim and Jeff Schroeder created Continuum (2022), a public artwork in Times Square that consisted of a 100 ft video wall emitting coloured lights and immersive healing sound frequencies. Let's create more public art that provides space for healing and safety.

Media architecture public policy must go beyond 'do no harm' and shifts to
'provide healing' for citizens. Human-centred cities can employ infrastructure,
architecture, and technology are tools to support them.

Spark the public imagination.

Bibliography

Levin, Sam. "New AI can guess whether you're gay or straight from a photograph." The
Guardian, September 7, 2017. https://www.theguardian.com/technology/2017/
sep/07/new-artificial-intelligence-can-tell-whether-youre-gay-or-straight-
from-a-photograph

Mullen, Jethro. "Virtual protest: Demonstrators challenge new law with holograms."
CNN. April 12, 2015. https://www.cnn.com/2015/04/12/europe/spain-holo-
gram-protest/index.html.
"Continuum." Toronto History Museums. https://www.toronto.ca/explore-enjoy/
history-art-culture/museums/continuum/.

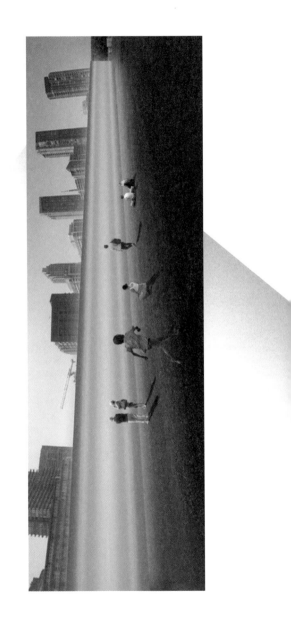

IMAGE DESCRIPTION: Continuum, at Fort York National Historic Site in Toronto, 2021. © Krista Kim and Jeff Schroeder

Anthea Foyer makes beautiful things using technology, compelling narratives across platforms, and starts conversations between strangers and friends – on and offline. She is a multi–disciplinary artist, storyteller, and curator of digital public art. She currently leads the Creative Technology office at the City of Toronto.

Anthea Foyer

RE:

Jiabao Li

Human perception has long been influenced by technological breakthroughs. An intimate mediation of technology lies in between our direct perceptions and the environment. Media architectures, ranging from personalized and individual spaces (phone screens, augmented reality glasses) to common and shared spaces (giant LED facades, light boxes), are shaping our sense of reality in invisible and nuanced ways. The vertical curation of media architecture means a single authority such as a government or corporation has control of the content. This can limit the scope of media architecture projects and the perspectives represented. I created a series of perceptual machines to help us defamiliarize and question the ways we see the mediated world.

We have observed an increase in allergies and intolerances in modern society. Hypersensitivities are emerging not only medically but also mentally. Media architecture reinforces people's tendency to overreact through the viral spread of information and amplification of opinions, making us hypersensitive to our sociopolitical environment. By creating an artificial allergy to the color red, Hyperallergic Vision *manifests the nonsensical hypersensitivity created by digital media. In nocebo mode, red expands, which is similar to social media's amplification effect; in placebo mode, red shrinks, like our filtered communication landscape where we can unfollow people with different opinions.*

Our perception is not only part of our identities, but also part of the value chain. Our visual field is packed with so much information that our perception has

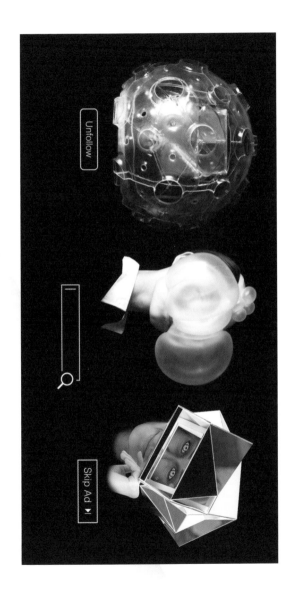

become a commodity with real estate value.

Designs are used to exploit our unconscious biases, algorithms favor content that reaffirms our opinions so that every little corner of our field of view is being colonized to sell ads. By creating tension between the meditative state and the consumptive state, Commoditized Vision *contemplates how our perception has become part of the value chain in this particular socioeconomic context. The viewer can earn money by looking at advertisements and spend money to see an ads-free world. Everyday activities are hampered because one has to turn vision into a money-making enterprise. Once the media is able to colonize our body, we have no choice anymore. The more efficient viewer becomes the more efficient laborer.*

Jiabao Li is an Assistant Professor of Design at The University of Texas at Austin and a Harvard graduate. She creates works addressing climate change, interspecies co-creation, humane technology, and perceptions. In Jiabao's TED Talk, she uncovered how technology mediates the way we perceive reality. Jiabao is the recipient of numerous awards including Forbes China 30 Under 30, and her work has been exhibited internationally, at Venice Architecture Biennale, Ars Electronica, Today Art Museum Biennial, SIGGRAPH, Milan and Dubai Design Week, ISEA, Anchorage Museum, and Museum of Design.

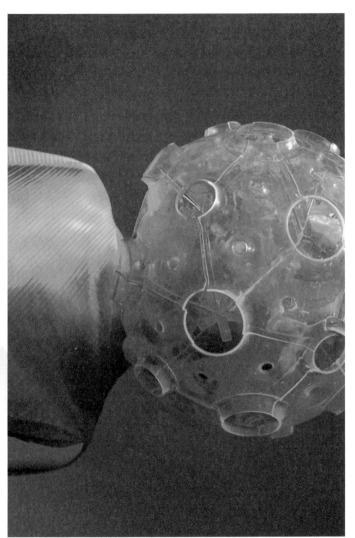

RE:

Matt Nish-Lapidus

On the train I take a moment to answer email, pre-order refreshments for the flight, and watch a failed attempt to make unreasonably ornate cookies. Arriving at the airport I really need a coffee. The café's ordering terminal is down for maintenance and the single staff member seems disinterested. The screens above the counter, usually displaying rotating seasonal menus, are broken. Each display is like an oil slick, the unhappy rainbow of colours digitally seeping into one another. Approaching the bar, the lone barista gestures at a QR code hastily taped to the countertop. I take out my mobile device and aim the camera. It takes a few tries to lock onto the QR code and open the url, which redirects to the café's app in the app store. I ask if I can order a drink but the barista says 'you have to order online' because the local systems are down, as indicated by the status display. I mill around uneasily, slowly becoming late for my flight. The barista smiles hesitantly at me and hands me a coffee, on the house. There is no functional system to record the transaction, so they take the opportunity to exercise what little agency they have. I can see my name materializing on the highly visible these-people-will-potentially-delay-the-flight display near the gate. Stepping away, my watch registers that I'm near the café and suggests I might like a coffee, inclu- ding a one-time discount code—just order at the terminal.

Matt Nish-Lapidus' varied practice probes the myth that computers should be useful rather than beautiful through examining contemporary technoculture and its histories, politics, and impacts. His work results in diverse outputs including publications, recordings, installations, performances, software, and objects. Matt has performed and exhibited with ACUD Macht Neu, Electric Eclectics, MOCA Toronto, InterAccess, ZKM, and more, including many DIY community spaces. You can find Matt online and away-from-keyboard under various aliases and collaborations including emenel, New Tendencies, and <blink>.

RE:

Ana Tobin

Trust. Is every experience designed in your best interest? Do you trust that a designer's influence isn't biased? That they have considered people with differing abilities? Too often, they have not.

Designed experiences connect us to our institutions, cities, communities, and even passersby. Map apps tell us the fastest route. Lighted pathways guide us in the park. Every waking moment, we are influenced by designers. Unintentional or not, designers omit the vastness of human experience, bodies, and minds. Designers need to consider all who interact with our designed experiences.

The multi-modality of media architecture bridges design for the differently abled and neurodivergent, but we must go beyond. We must co-create with all our users and consider our designs incomplete until they are accessible. We must engage with our marginalized communities and know the range of our audience. To do this, we can borrow tactics from social design, get communities involved in the design process, and borrow from UX/UI design and engage in user testing.

Let us expand our growing use of multi-modal designs. In Alejandro G. Iñárritu's Carne y Arena *experience, users stand shoeless in a cold sandy warehouse armed with a backpack and VR headset. They simulate crossing the US-Mexico border while patrol agents point guns. This example is grand, but most experience is granular. A smaller scale example is to use accessible typefaces like Atkinson Hyperlegible from the Braille Institute, which helps those with vision im-*

pairment and shows potential for reading-based learning disabilities. A typeface is a small yet practical change and a deeply effective one.

I challenge designers to engage with a realistic community, not an idealized one. To (Dis)Engage with the idea of an average human. To consider all who will interact with our work to enable meaningful experiences accessible to all.

Atkinson Hyprlegible

A typeface created by the Braille Institute for low vision readers, but may also help this with reading based learning disabilities because each character is unique

"p" overlaid on "b" → "d" overlaid on "p" → "b" overlaid on "d" →

bed

b p d

ABCDEFGHIJKLMNOPQRSTUVWXYZ
abcdefghijklmnopqrstuvwxyz1234567890

Ana Tobin is a multimedia designer and educator. She received her B.F.A. in graphic design and her B.S. in advertising from Boston University and her M.F.A. in Graphic Design from Maryland Institute College of Art. Her work focuses primarily on experiential graphic design with accessibility at its core. Prior to graduate school, she worked for a non-profit, at a print and web design firm, and at an environmental and exhibition design firm. She is currently an Assistant Professor of Graphic Design at George Mason University and a freelance designer.

The Empire State Building is one of the most photographed buildings in the world due in no small part to its frequently changing lighting programs. The ease in which images can be captured and circulated, constituting new on-screen and off-screen spaces, illustrates the complexity of the cultural, commercial, and ideological goals that drive image circulation more generally. The Empire State Building and other examples of media architecture also feature prominently in videos promoting tourism and migration, music videos, and films.

What are the historical, contemporary, and future relationships between media architecture and its related images, and what is at stake in these processes? What are the mechanics and politics of media architectural remediation?

PROVOCATION:
Collage offers new understandings of images and forms
through juxtapositions and adjacencies.

What is a collage of media architecture?*

* Following the MAB23 theme *Intermedial Media Architecture*

RE:

Susan Blight

Mii o'ow igo mewinzha ...(1)

*Do you remember the wood collages made by Waawaatay'gonegaabo (2),
standing in the Northern Lights recreating the Lake Superior shoreline piece by
piece? That wood collage-art preparators always said it was heavy- was never
distanced from Land. By Land we mean, land/water/air/subterranean earth (3)
and the memory created within. They say he made these pieces because he was
homesick(4) for anishinaabewi-gichigami (5) so, there is a longing within the
action of collage and a memory. He called that horizon line a point of departure.
A point of departure is where you start.*

*Collage can be a presence in absence. It can be "make do with what you have"
but also "make it yours and in your style." A cut out, a paste or a replace consti-
tutes an erasure. It is a remix to create possibility. Or a shift, to go from the old
to the new and the newer. But you still honour its old form. How you honour it is
up to you. As Tina M. Campt writes in* Listening to Images, *quiet must not be con-
flated with silence. Quiet registers in the body as a haptic. So, in the making of
the in-between of media and architecture- the sliding of one form into another
and across and underneath- what are the sounds we feel as we are departing
and starting?*

Endnotes

1. "It used to be this way long ago..."

2. George Morrison.

3. Tuck, Eve and K. Wayne Yang, "Decolonization is not a Metaphor." Decolonization: Indigeneity, Education & Society 1, no.1 (2012): 1-40.

4. John Haworth writing in American Indian Magazine, states that the origin of George Morrison's wood collages "lay in his homesickness for the Lake Superior shore and his childhood habit of beachcombing."

5. Lake Superior.

Susan Blight (Anishinaabe, Couchiching First Nation) is an interdisciplinary artist working with public art, site-specific intervention, film and social practice. Her solo and collaborative work engages questions of personal and cultural identity and its relationship to space. Susan is Chair in Indigenous Visual Culture at Ontario College of Art & Design University and an Assistant Professor in the Faculty of Arts &Science.

Susan Blight

RE:

John Cayley

The medium shared by entities across media architectures is language, prompting a singular generative relation. Call it reading – *scanning or hearing linguistic images, graphic and acoustic, so as to reembody significance and affect – something, to our knowledge, only human animals can achieve. Readable traces of language have their own architecture. They engage differentially with at least three categories of media architecture: built, software, and virtual. Software architectures develop and reconfigure at high speeds with little regard for built architectures, unless, in late capitalism, both are co-opted and vectored by profitable commerce. Virtual architectures tend to simulate or augment what has been built and reproduce spaces where signage or captioning are the only affordances of language which are deployed effectively and in harmony with virtual architecture. Software architectures nonetheless have the potential to extend and reconfigure linguistic affordances. The built and the virtual, however, are not yet* medial *for these potential relations; they are either 'in the way' or else they offer more or less unreadable spaces. Peripheral theaters and spectacles are 'tacked' on or into built environments rather than integrated as places to live, converse, and read. Think of the 'multimedia boxes' inside larger public cultural venues, otherwise brilliantly architected. XR, Extended Reality (encompassing Virtual and Augmented), may offer reconfiguration when not subservient to what is built. Software architectures – those which engage with media and including those which generate what we describe as Virtual – must slow down and converse with culturally attuned built developments. As an example of what might be done, consider* aurality, *the world of sound, especially linguistic sound, which com-*

plements visuality. Since language is not just text, spatially articulated aurality in the built environment calls out for more and more imaginative exploration.

John Cayley is a maker of language art in programmable media. Along with poetry and translation, he has explored dynamic and ambient poetics, heuristic text generation, transliteral morphing, aestheticized vectors of reading, and transactive synthetic language. Academically, he investigates the ontology of language in the context of philosophically informed practice-based research. Professor of Literary Arts at Brown University, his publications include *Grammalepsy: Selected Essays on Digital Language Art*, and *Image Generation* from counterpathpress. org. His own site is programmatology.com.

RE:

The Current Team

Provides Ng, Artem Konevskikh, Eli Joteva, Ya Nzi, and GPT2

Prologue

Current is now, the inevitable flows and trends, it's the drifts and shifts, it's the livestream of data. The Current Team conducted this piece of provocation, supervised by AI, which transformed the collective intelligence of philosophers and their writings to juxtapose urban urgencies and adjacencies - a collage of media architecture.

=====

Urban urgency nowadays is the need for a meaningful way of life. There is however another way, what we have called ecologically-based lifestyles, which are fundamentally based on justice and on sharing with others. In this sense, we can say that the current ecological crisis is, at the same time, a social crisis in human history, it is as if humans have turned their back on a crucial part of their identity. It is imperative to change our way of life - urban urgency resides in the parameters of social problems.

The Frankfurt school, which attracted a large number of intellectuals, historians and anthropologists in the mid-twentieth century called itself the materialist school, encouraging a socio-critical approach to ecology that believed humans were vivacious, ephemeral and enduring. In contrast, the anthropological cultural tradition of the school believed in a justice based on individual rights. The theory of social interaction is conditioned by the epistemology of identities of the social world, but in order to gain insight into the nature of social interaction, it is necessary to make a separation between the perception of the social world and

IMAGE 1 DESCRIPTION he urban reality is an ammalgation of everyday objects, planning intentions, and instances of social encounters. 'Unreal Cheung Sha Wan' by Clara Keqing Jiao, Dining Liu, Genie Ng, Jessica Wong, Kiko So, Lexie Liang, Stanley Leung, Zita Cheung – 'Volumetric Cinema' Workshop by Current.cam & R.E.Ar_ at UABB 2022.

no matter how much one may want to point the fingers of criticism at the wrong actors, the constructive question is how we can live, together. We live in such a complex world, in which much of the social infrastructure is not only produced, but often distorted by misunderstanding and miscommunication, and the misbelief to overpower other cultures and their histories in assisting them to become more civilised and democratic. The argument about crisis can be framed in two ways: 'It's on my mind, it's not on your mind; it's on my phone, it's not on my car; it's not on the subway, it's not on the plane, it's not at work. It is like being aware of what is not on your mind, and Steps to an Ecology of Mind.'
– The Generative Pretrained Transformer

The first half of our answer means, in effect, to ask: What does human life consist of in all its intensity? What does human society consist of in all its structure? Even in the second half: What is human contact? What does 'human' mean? How to make it human? What does it mean to be human? We face the same problem.

References:

GPT2 models
Radford, A. (2019). *Better language models and their implications*. OpenAI. Retrieved May 13, 2022, from https://openai.com/blog/better-language-models/
Radford, A., Wu, J., Child, R., Luan, D., Amodei, D., & Sutskever, I. (2019). Language models are unsupervised multi task learners. OpenAI blog, 1(8), 9. https://cdn.openai.com/better-language-models/language_models_are_unsupervised_multit ask_learners.pdf

Late Philosopher Books used to train GPT2
Bateson, G. (1972). *Steps to an ecology of mind collected essays in anthropology, psychiatry, evolution, and epistemology*. Chandler.
Benjamin, W. (1935). The Work of Art in the Age of Mechanical Reproduction, 1936. Fisher, M., & Davies, S. (2009). *Capitalist realism: Is there no alternative?* Zero Books. Foucault, M. (1966). *The Order of Things: An Archaeology of the Human Sciences*.
Lévy, P. (1997) Collective Intelligence: Mankind's Emerging World in Cyberspace. New York: Plenum Press
Marx, K. (1858). Fragment on machines. The grundrisse, 690-712.
Nash Jr, J. F. (2008). The agencies method for modeling coalitions and cooperation in games. International Game Theory Review, 10(04), 539-564.
Radford, A. (2019). *Better language models and their implications*. OpenAI. Retrieved May 13, 2022, from https://openai.com/blog/better-language-models/
Virilio, P. (1986). *Speed and politics: An essay on dromology*. Columbia University.
Wiener, N. (1950). *The human use of human beings, cybernetics and society. Norbert Wiener* .. Houghton Mifflin Co.

Current is an interdisciplinary-intercultural collective working at the intersection of art, architecture, and technology. Through the medium of volumetric cinema, Current delineates the multiplicity of futures in the attention economy and its material manifestations.

Current was founded by Provides Ng, Eli Joteva, Ya Nzi, and Artem Konevskikh; 'The Current Team' denotes its broader network of Creative Commons (www.current.cam). Current has been exhibiting and teaching worldwide, including Rijksmuseum Twenthe, Bartlett UCL, UCLA Sci|Art Lab, and more.

RE:

Sherry Dobbin

'...radical proposition is a practice of magical manufacture which takes cultural expressions delimited in a quagmire of authentic realness, isolated purity and self-contained genesis, and unleashes them in an entirely new direction, an entirely new mode...'
– Adrienne Edwards on Wangechi Mutu (2014).

Rauschenberg combined found object and artistic stroke, dismantling fine art hierarchy. Deborah Roberts' collages give her subjects 'character and agency to find their own way amidst the complicated narratives...'' Laurie Anderson pioneered music and art as equal contenders into the populist form of video. The Cubists purposefully outlined the viewer's act as the work's completion, bringing the 'everyman' into 'genius' domain.

Robert Wilson taught me that site-specific work empowers everyone as powerful collaborators in an open-ended durational work of multiple (un)controlled narratives. Referencing that collaborative curatorial approach, which I employed at Times Square Arts, I titled my 2016 Moscow exhibition Times Square(d): Theater of the Absurd. *Like characters awaiting* Godot, *or stuck in* Huis Clos, *or expecting* The Rhinoceros, *people gather at city centres to participate in a collage drama that unfolds in the 'waiting for ...'*

Seven years on, 'cities as sets of absurdist drama' isn't radical; it resonates globally. Digital media within architecture (outdoor advertising, integrated design façade, transportation infrastructure) has accelerated the transformation of static, authorial architecture into solicitous, dynamic structures that require individuals' interactions to complete themselves. Through further interface of portable technology, there's a practice (or responsibility) for all to actively collage both additive content creation and subtractive editing. Virtual participants are invited to join the space; duration is malleable and individually controlled; framing is infinite.

We, the Cyborg Citizens, are characters and authors of multimedia opera, creators of new absurdist drama, conductors of collage where media fluidity is permanently embedded into architecture.

– SRD, 2 Jan 2023

＊ Deborah Roberts, "Artist Statement," http://www.deborahrobertsart.com/artist-statement.

Sherry Dobbin is an international cultural advisor working between cities, real estate and the cultural sector to embed forward-looking cultural infrastructure with new financial modes. She is curatorial founder of *Midnight Moment* and past Director at *Times Square Arts* and *The Watermill Center*. When Partner at Futurecity, she brokered Centre Pompidou for STH_BNK by Beulah; Royal Philharmonic Orchestra for Wembley Park; digital archivists for Museum of London; affordable XR studios; digital heritage centre; and wrote *The Reel Store* feasibility study.

Sherry Dobbin

IMAGE 1 DESCRIPTION: June 2016, Midnight Moment in Times Square, NYC. Alex Prager's Applause, 2016. Photo credit Ka-Man Tse for Times Square Arts.

RE:

Scott Rodgers

Social media platforms process and display voluminous and varied images of the city, so they can make peculiar collages of media ar,,chitecture. Their users are not so unlike Robert Rauschenberg, collating found urban objects, images and words into combines. Smartphones on the ready, social media users snap, edit and tag photos of themselves, banal objects and various urban situations. They re-share and modify screenshots, memes, stock photos and design visualizations.

Using tools like ImagePlot, researchers, including me, have made analytic collages with scraped, sorted and visualized social media images of the city. Shown here is a cropped render of 4733 Twitter images related to a controversial East London cycling infrastructure scheme, plotting (along polar coordinates) brightness against saturation. Clustered adjacencies of grey-toned images show asphalt, stone paving slabs and dark anthracite bollards. Juxtaposed images show reddish-orange construction barriers, yellow construction notices, red bike lanes, green bicycle storage sheds and white screengrabs. Do such academic visualizations resemble the urban collage experienced by the social media user? No, not quite. Social media platforms tend to deliver images via time-based streams modulated by algorithmic rankings of 'relevance', determined using interactional metadata about relationships between different users and what they post, share, like, tag and more. In this way, social platforms produce 'combines' of urban images from various times and places, which appear differentially to subsets of people inhabiting particular moments, places or settings, and performing various norms, practices and impulses. Visualizations like this one instead offer us a

further analytic collage, extracting found urban images from stream-based plat-
forms, and re-collating them to discover patterns among the images themselves.

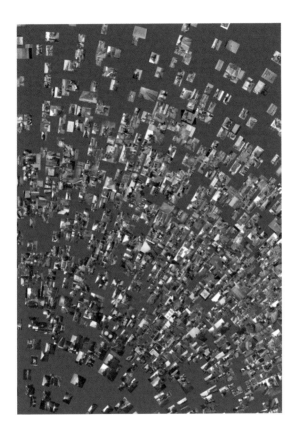

Scott Rodgers is Reader in Media and Geography at Birkbeck, University of London. His current research focuses on how digital platforms reshape contemporary urbanism and politics. He has recently studied how everyday and profes-
sionalized uses of social media platforms remediate how publics experience and
articulate urban transformation. Scott is also in the early stages of exploring the
relationships between the layered aesthetics of London's King's Cross redevelopment and platform companies relocating to the area.

RE:

Anna Weisling

*When the doors of shared spaces closed in 2020, performers faced a harsh re-
ality: stages were few and far between, and the closest, biggest one was online.
Existential questions loomed–if you translate performance through a network,
what comes out on the other side?*

SHP of THSEUS *is a collaborative work developed by RE/SHFT/ER, an ensemble
of interdisciplinary performers located across the U.S. Conceptualized during the
pandemic, the piece takes inspiration from Greek legend: Theseus, journeying at
sea, gradually replaces parts of his ship, one by one, until nothing of the original
remains.*

In SHP, *musicians work with both sound and control signals; each instrument
produces sound, but its controls can also be influenced by others. Each performer
follows a palindromic score (A-B-C-C-B-A) that is randomly generated from a
bank of 10 images at the start of each performance. Performers interpret these
images (which were sketched in advance by each member) through improvi-
sed musical gestures and formal decisions throughout the piece. The original
sketches were also used to construct a set of 3-dimensional objects for the visual
elements of the piece; during performance, a camera captures the objects in re-
al-time and sends the video feed to a computer, which processes the image into
3D geometry. These digital recreations can then be manipulated further–each
step of the process revealing itself as it broadcasts outward. Connective threads
between music, image, and meaning are continually woven and undone.*

SHP *has been performed both nationally and internationally, but as we return to our shared spaces it will soon face an identity crisis of its own: If you remove the network from a network performance, is it still the same?*

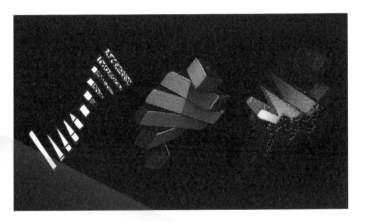

Anna Weisling is a practice-based researcher whose interests include music, interaction design, and visual performance. She is currently an Assistant Professor in the Emerging Technology in Business + Design department at Miami University in Oxford, Ohio. www.aweisling.com

RE/SHFT/ER is Nick Hwang, Eric Sheffield, Anthony T. Marasco, Jeff Herriott, and Anna Weisling.

Digital Mediation, A Wish List

From the frustratingly disjunctive experience of waiting in line for coffee at an airport café, small-scale and fleeting, to the willful defamiliarization of an entire urban context by wearing blob-like helmets, to its pursuant reclamation through graffiti art and assemblages of social media, the mediation of urban and architectural space through digital technologies finally folds over onto itself. It reconciles with its own consequences in order to move through the critical reconditioning charged by the social, political, and economic contexts of now.

Viewed through the lens of the twenty-one contributions above, this digital mediation thus undergoes a massive shift, not tech-centric in moving to higher resolution displays or novel implementations of technologies (although certainly these shifts continue), but rather towards the self-reflective, looking intensely outwards to systemic context in order to look inwards.

It could be proposed, then, that this moment of re-mediation asks for a set of goals, a sort of wish list*, or, aptly, a delineation of provocations with which to carry into further practice.

If this is the case, it might read something like:

If digital technologies are to mediate urban and architectural space,
     remember there is no singular or homogenous public, but publics.
If digital technologies are to mediate urban and architectural space,
     re-vector the dynamic for each of those publics.
If digital technologies are to mediate urban and architectural space,
     carry respect for those who let us, or our work, into their homes.
If digital technologies are to mediate urban and architectural space,
     enable quiet togetherness, or quiet aloneness, but never silent isolation.
If digital technologies are to mediate urban and architectural space,

slow technology to architecture's relationship with time.

If digital technologies are to mediate urban and architectural space,
give architecture a fast-paced animated boost.

If digital technologies are to mediate urban and architectural space,
take on long-standing hegemonies.

If digital technologies are to mediate urban and architectural space,
give way to empowered and just encounters.

If digital technologies are to mediate urban and architectural space,
remember routine begins with simple repetitive acts.

If digital technologies are to mediate urban and architectural space,
transcend physical typologies in their translation to the virtual.

If digital technologies are to mediate urban and architectural space,
delve into historical pluralities.

If digital technologies are to mediate urban and architectural space,
allow technology to combust.

If digital technologies are to mediate urban and architectural space,
close your eyes and experience it again.

If digital technologies are to mediate urban and architectural space,
embrace shadow, and beautiful tension.

If digital technologies are to mediate urban and architectural space,
heal.

If digital technologies are to mediate urban and architectural space,
seek liminalities and interstices.

If digital technologies are to mediate urban and architectural space,
speak for the nonhuman.

If digital technologies are to mediate urban and architectural space,
consider legibility, of text, of experience.

If digital technologies are to mediate urban and architectural space,
challenge the relationship between media consumption and labor.

If digital technologies are to mediate urban and architectural space,
hear the buzzing, the multitudes of technological contexts already at play.

If digital technologies are to mediate urban and architectural space,

Ian Callender and Annie Dell'Aria

engender thoughtfulness, which sometimes does not mean ease of use.

If digital technologies are to mediate urban and architectural space,

let go, and slip between space and time.

If digital technologies are to mediate urban and architectural space,

show your hand; show your motives.

If digital technologies are to mediate urban and architectural space,

design for misuse, for uncertainty, and for shifts in context.

If digital technologies are to mediate urban and architectural space,

illuminate new perceptions.

If digital technologies are to mediate urban and architectural space,

find knowledge in creative destruction.

If digital technologies are to mediate urban and architectural space,

perceive air as but one container of space.

If digital technologies are to mediate urban and architectural space,

juxtapose, or place adjacent. Centralize the peripheral.

If digital technologies are to mediate urban and architectural space,

be realistic about what's within your control.

If digital technologies are to mediate urban and architectural space,

understand that your control is infinite.

If digital technologies are to mediate urban and architectural space,

engage the haptic and aural.

If digital technologies are to mediate urban and architectural space,

fold work over on itself; test the reality it figures forth.

If digital technologies are to mediate urban and architectural space,

remember that this work carries real meaning and purpose.

*Format of a "Wish List" after Hilary Sample, "IF HOUSING THEN...A WISH LIST." In Michael Maltzan, Social Transparency: Projects on Housing. New York: Columbia Books on Architecture and the City, 2016.

Ian Callender is a New York City-based multidisciplinary artist and designer exploring the intersection of the built environment and digital technologies. His work has been recognized by, among others, the Architizer A+ Awards, the SEGD Global Design Awards, and the ADC Awards; presented at conferences such as the International Symposium on Electronic Art and the Media Architecture Biennale; published in ArchDaily, Hyperallergic, and MIT's *Thresholds*; and exhibited internationally.

Annie Dell'Aria is an Associate Professor of Art History at Miami University in Oxford, Ohio, USA. Her research concerns the intersection of moving image media, contemporary art, and public space. She is the author of *The Moving Image as Public Art: Sidewalk Spectators and Modes of Enchantment* (Palgrave Macmillan, 2021) as well as articles and chapters in journals and edited volumes in both art history and media studies. She is Co-Chair of the organization Public Art Dialogue.

Set Margins' #19

Provocations on Media Architecture

Editors
Ian Callender and Annie Dell'Aria

Publisher
Set Margins' publications

Graphic Designer
Freek Lomme

Producer
Dave Colangelo

With the support of the Social Sciences and Humanities Research Council of Canada